Original title:

Defining Life with a Question Mark

Author: Eleanor Prescott

ISBN HARDBACK: 978-1-80566-022-4

ISBN PAPERBACK: 978-1-80566-317-1

How Can Questions Illuminate the Path?

What's that buzzing in my ear?
Is it wisdom or just fear?
Why do socks always disappear?
Should I have had that extra beer?

Why does my cat stare at the wall?
Is he waiting for a grand ball?
Do plants ever feel small?
Will I trip if I don't crawl?

Can I twirl in a grocery store?
Will the cashier give a roar?
Why can't I ever find the door?
Is that my phone, or just folklore?

Do clouds ever wear a frown?
Can they dance with the wind around?
Why do clowns wear such a crown?
What if laughter is profound?

When Life Meets Its Mystique

Why do socks always disappear?
Did they travel to a land of cheer?
With cups that dance and spoons that sing,
Where lost things gather for a fling?

A cat that thinks it's a tiny king,
And chairs that creak when you start to swing.
Life's odd puzzles, oh what a jest,
Yet somehow, we find it's the best!

The Intersection of Reason and Question.

Where do the queries take a stroll?
In a park where doubts make a mole?
With sights unseen and sounds unclear,
Do we tiptoe or shout, 'Come here!'?

A chicken crossing, or just a riddle?
Is it funny, or are we just twiddlin'?
Around the bend where giggles grow,
Life's sense of humor just steals the show!

Seeking Clarity in Shadows

Under a lamp that flickers bright,
I ponder mysteries into the night.
Do shadows plot, with secrets they keep?
Or just hang around, avoiding sleep?

A ghost that swoops with a loopy grin,
Trying to dance but wears a bin.
Life's quirky ways make my head spin,
In shadows, I find my laughter within!

What Colors the Uncertain Sky?

Is the sky a canvas, oh so bold?
With crayons of laughter, stories told?
I ask the clouds, do they ever frown?
Or just float by, wearing their crown?

Maybe it's paint from sunsets last,
Or sprinkles from a birthday blast.
So many shades, it's hard to guess,
In this world, it's quite the mess!

The Weight of Curious Hearts

Why do we ponder the stars above?
When ants just march, in search of love?
Do socks get lonely when they lose their pair?
Or do they plot revenge from the laundry chair?

What's under the bed that we fear at night?
Sometimes it's just a shoe, not a fright.
Do pillows dream of all our thoughts?
Or simply wonder where all our socks are lost?

How Do We Paint the Invisible?

If clouds wear hats, what do they choose?
Do rainbows giggle at their colorful hues?
Can silence be loud, or is it just shy?
And does the moon envy the sun in the sky?

Do crayons whisper secrets in a box?
Or do they just chatter like curious fox?
Can a whisper dance if the wind sings too?
While little stars wink, saying, 'We see you!'

The Sound of Unarticulated Dreams

What noise does a wish make when it flies?
Is it a giggle or just soft sighs?
Do shoes argue over which path to take?
Or do they just dance, for the journey's sake?

If laughter were a fruit, how sweet would it be?
Would it roll down the hill, just to see?
Do forks feel unused when leftovers stay cold?
Or do they rejoice, feeling quite bold?

Are We the Questions We Carry?

Do we ask ourselves, what's for dinner this time?
As if our lives need a rhythm or rhyme?
Is a cat a philosopher when it stares at the wall?
Or is it just plotting its next great fall?

Why do we worry about things yet to be?
When a ticklish belly can promise a spree?
Can a sneeze be the answer we seek in disguise?
Does curiosity wear a pair of bright eyes?

The Journey Beyond the Conundrum

In a world of whys and hows,
We stumble through like clumsy cows.
Are we all just cosmic jokes?
Punchlines whispered by the folks?

Laughter echoes through the night,
As stars twinkle with delight.
Is every answer just a grin?
Wait, where did my thought begin?

With each step, a riddle toss,
Do we work or just play boss?
Reality feels like a game,
But who will take the blame?

So here we dance on this tightrope,
Juggling dreams, a twist of hope.
In this circus, we're the clowns,
Wearing joy like silly crowns.

Questions Wrapped in Time

Tick tock goes the clock, so grand,
What's the secret of this land?
Is tomorrow really just today?
Or do our plans just go astray?

In a coffee shop, I ask my brew,
"Do you think that life's a zoo?"
It gives a nod, and I just sigh,
Maybe it's the latte high?

While staring at the moonlit pond,
I ponder all the questions spawned.
Are ducks in formation on a quest?
To find the best spot for a rest?

With every giggle, time unwinds,
Amidst confusion, joy finds.
So let's embrace this wacky ride,
And smile before our thoughts subside.

Is Existence a Shared Dream?

When I wake, is it all a prank?
Are we the goldfish in a tank?
With bubbles swirling, thoughts like foam,
Is the universe our shared home?

Chatting with my cat at dawn,
"Is life a dream, or just a yawn?"
He blinks and yawns, then scurries by,
Does he know more than you or I?

We dance on paths of cosmic schemes,
Are they nightmares or wild dreams?
In each laugh, our worries fade,
Is sanity just an outdated trade?

So let's toast to our whims today,
With questions that wiggle and sway.
Are we the punchline or the joke?
Here's to truth wrapped in smoke!

A Journey Paved by Wonder

In a forest of curious thoughts,
Do I cherish what I've sought?
Every twist in this mental maze,
Is it clever? Just a phase?

As rain drops down like Twitter feeds,
Got questions blooming like wild weeds.
What's the meaning behind a bird's song?
Could it be we've all been wrong?

In traffic jams of inner strife,
I laugh at the chaos called "life."
Is each honk a question, yes or no?
Why do we drive so fast, then slow?

So take a moment, pause and grin,
The journey's wild, let's dive in!
With oddities and charming quirks,
Let's find joy in all that works.

The Canvas of Wonder

Why do socks go missing?
Is it part of a grand scheme?
Do they dance in the shadows?
Or maybe they just dream?

Do we really need to know?
When the world is a surprise?
Like a cat in a top hat,
With secrets in its eyes.

What's peeking from the fridge?
Is it leftover spaghetti?
Or a science experiment?
Oh, it's gone all confetti!

Is cereal a soup?
Or just breakfast in disguise?
Do we sip or do we chew?
The truth, oh how it flies!

Life's Unfinished Sentences

I ordered a salad, but...
Can I substitute fries?
Do they come with a caution?
Or just more buttery lies?

If time flies like a plane,
What happens when it lands?
Does it gather its baggage?
Or shake out its hands?

Can a fish learn to dance?
Or does it just wiggle and sway?
Is an octopus confused?\nOr knows how to play?

What's the sound of one clapping?
Does it echo in the air?
Or does it just leave silence?
With a questioning glare?

The Puzzle of Our Path

If life is a puzzle, then...
What piece do I employ?
Do I grab the edges first?
Or just hunt for the toy?

Where do all the socks go?
In realms of make-believe?
Do they form a union?
Or just plot and weaves?

If I trip on a banana,
Is it fate or pure fun?
Is the peel a warning sign?
Or just a joke on the run?

Where's the treasure I seek?
Is it in the fridge cold?
Or do I find some wisdom,
In tales that are told?

A Journey Through Uncertainty

Is life a roller coaster?
Or just a lazy stream?
Do we scream from the high parts?
Or sip tea and just dream?

When life gives you lemons,
Do you barter for a pie?
Or juggle them like pros?
As the neighbors walk by?

If laughter is the answer,
What was the question then?
Is it all just a riddle?
Or a game for us, friends?

Do we dance with the unknown?
Or run away in fright?
In the chaos, let's chuckle,
And just enjoy the plight!

When Is a Choice Not a Choice?

Do I want coffee or tea,
Or just an old cup of glee?
What's better, a cat or a dog?
Why does it feel like a fog?

I choose between socks or shoes,
But end up with mismatched blues.
Salad or pie, what shall I eat?
Did I just lose to my own feat?

A decision with every bite,
Should I dance or just hold tight?
With choices littered all around,
My mind's a circus, joy unbound.

Fragments of Forgotten Thoughts

What color was that dress I wore?
Was it blue or shades of folklore?
Did I eat lunch or skip the day?
My brain's a puzzle in dismay.

Thoughts bubble up like boiling tea,
Yet, most are just too hard to see.
Did I lock the door or simply dream?
Life's a stage, or so it seems.

Memories drift like autumn leaves,
Twirling, swirling, catching thieves.
I search for answers with great flair,
Only to find, they're not quite there.

Where Do Questions Lead the Heart?

Where does a 'why' lead, I ponder,
Does it take me yonder, fonder?
If I ask if I asked it right,
Will the sun come back tonight?

Do questions bounce like a rubber ball?
Or do they fade into the hall?
Can I question if questions are true?
Oh dear, what will I do?

With every 'what' and 'how' I say,
I wander further from the way.
Yet giggles sprout like flowers rare,
A heart's confusion light as air.

The Riddle of the Mind's Eye

What does my mind see when it spins?
A race of thoughts or silly grins?
An elephant wearing polka dots?
Or a chicken with oversized crocs?

If I squint hard, will it get clear?
Or will it vanish, poor dear?
Do my visions dance or just sit tight?
A question mark under moonlight.

Should I follow where my thoughts lead?
Or let them roam and plant a seed?
With riddles floating on the breeze,
My brain's a circus, if you please.

Searching for Light in Dusk's Embrace

In shadows dance the fireflies' way,
Are they lost or just here to play?
With each flash, a secret we seek,
Do they know what we dare not speak?

The sun says goodbye with a wink,
But stars giggle, teasing us to think.
Do they argue over who shines bright?
Or is it just a cosmic light fight?

Clouds in a huddle, whisper with glee,
Are they planning a joke for you and me?
As twilight wraps the world in gray,
Could it be night's version of day?

With each dusk, a puzzle unfolds,
What tales of wonder can dusk hold?
In this charm of a fading hue,
Is laughter life's riddle, too?

Is Everything a Metaphor?

Honey drips from my morning tea,
Is it sweet or just meant to be?
A spoonful of wisdom in my cup,
Or just the sugar I slurp up?

Life's questions spin like a top,
Do we laugh, or is it all a flop?
With each quirk, a deeper dive,
Is the answer simply 'to survive'?

The cat on the fence, proud and grand,
Is he pondering life or just his band?
With every meow, he claims his throne,
Are we all just cats, feeling alone?

Balloons drift up, chasing the sky,
Do they wonder how or why?
As they pop with a giggle and cheer,
Is the burst just a joke, I fear?

What Notes Does Life Play in Silence?

In stillness, a symphony waits,
Does silence hold all the fates?
A whisper of secrets hums through the air,
Is it music or just a dare?

Crickets chirp in the night's soft wrap,
Are they in tune or stuck in a trap?
With each note that floats away,
Do we dance to what they say?

The clock ticks loud, in a comedic way,
Is time laughing or just in a play?
Every tick a giant jest,
Does it know we're on our quest?

In the hush where dreams do sway,
Are we listening or gone astray?
With a wink, the night takes flight,
Is silence the punchline of our plight?

Climbing the Mountain of Doubt

Up the hill, my thoughts do climb,
Is this mountain made of rhyme?
With each step, do questions shout,
Is the answer buried in doubt?

I slip and slide on a bath of fear,
Do I shout or just lend an ear?
Incredulous thoughts pull me down,
Are they just clowns in a great big gown?

Peeking over the ledge with a grin,
Is the view worth all this spin?
With clouds teasing, a jest they shout,
Do heights just lead to further bout?

Alpine air is crisp and clear,
Does my worry disappear here?
With laughter echoing all about,
Is the climb just a roundabout?

Questioning the Breath of Days

Is breakfast really the most?
What if lunch just wants a boast?
The clock ticks on, a teasing game,
Tick-tock, is it all the same?

Should socks match, or do they dare?
Can chips and dip be quite a pair?
Life's a riddle dressed in fluff,
Do we know when we've had enough?

When does a nap become a snooze?
Is snoozing just what we choose?
Chasing daydreams on a whim,
Or just a rest for folks like him?

With giggles hidden in each turn,
Do lessons stop, or ever learn?
At times, it feels like blissful jest,
Ah, the questions, aren't they the best?

Beyond the Horizon of Answers

What's that thing we chase each morn?
Is it caffeine or pure adorn?
If skies are blue, is that the prize?
Or just a canvas with surprise?

If clouds could dance, would they in glee?
What if trees talk back to me?
The sun winks down, a playful tease,
So many wonders in the breeze!

Is the moon shy, or just remote?
Does it laugh at our little boat?
Stars spark questions, twinkling reasons,
In silly times like holiday seasons!

As whims ebb and flow in tides,
We wonder on with smiles wide.
With laughter echoing far and near,
What a curious life we steer!

The Dance of Doubt

Do cats really hold the secret?
In dreams, they plot and then they edit!
When does one lose the perfect thread?
Or does it dance just in our head?

If bees could vote, what would they tell?
Would honey be their magic spell?
While ants march on in perfect lines,
Is chaos just a sign of signs?

What's the deal with socks that hide?
Do they conspire, take a ride?
Life's a jiggle, a curious spry,
Every question makes us sigh!

Each 'why' a step, a skip, a twirl,
In this dance, we all do whirl.
With chuckles loud, we doubt and play,
Oh, let's question life away!

When Purpose Meets Mystery

If toast could talk, would it say nice?
Or just complain about the slice?
And what of coffee's bold embrace?
Is it a hug? A morning race?

What's the story behind a sneeze?
A little magic or just bees?
Do plants sway to their own beat?
Do they enjoy a bit of heat?

Time's a puzzle, ticked alive,
Can questions help us truly thrive?
With laughter lit like fireflies,
Will we find truths in our whys?

Can giggles scratch the surface deep?
Will life reveal what we can keep?
As mysteries swirl like fizzy drinks,
Let's toast to doubts, what life thinks!

Dancing with the Unknown

In the kitchen, I trip on a shoe,
Making my dance moves seem far from true.
The fridge hums a tune, slightly off beat,
I laugh at my shadow, it just won't compete.

The cat joins the party, tail in the air,
With a prance and a twist, full of flair.
A tumble, a giggle, paint drops on the floor,
Who knew that life had such tricks in store?

Outer space beckons with odd little signs,
As I ponder the purpose of all these designs.
Is that a green alien? Or just a balloon?
I'll figure it out—after I vacuum the room.

With each little wobble, I embrace the whim,
Questions like confetti float out on a whim.
What if tomorrow brings rain, or some cake?
I dance with unknowns, make no mistake.

What Happens When We Ask?

What's the meaning of that squirrel's strange stare?
Does he contemplate life, or just snacks in the air?
I'll break out the cookies, take a seat on the swing,
Just what will I learn if I start asking things?

Why do ducks quack in perfect delight?
And why does the sun set on such a strange night?
If I ask a plant if it prefers sun or shade,
Will it grow me a secret? Or just leave me betrayed?

The toaster just popped, with a glow and a whirr,
I wondered aloud if it's mad at the blur.
Does it dream of more than just bread on the rack?
While pondering questions, the butter falls back.

So let's keep it light, oh, let's ride the breeze,
Asking the world, like we're eight years at ease.
What's with this giggle that follows my quest?
Life's just a party; let's figure the rest!

Layers of Meaning in a Simple Day

I poured my coffee, but it seemed quite a mess,
With creamer swirling like a satin dress.
I ponder the universe, even as I sip,
Why does my toast always want to flip?

The socks in the dryer play hide and seek,
They vanish like mysteries—oh, what a pique!
Do they dream of new lives with a cozy seat?
Or become lost adventurers wandering street?

The humor in traffic can lighten the load,
I chuckle at folks with their phones on the road.
Is that person dancing or just caught in a glitch?
With each quirky gesture, I laugh and I twitch.

Today as I wander, I'll ask but won't fret,
With layers of meaning, there's no need to sweat.
What's truly important? The fun—and the flow!
Life's almost a riddle, but I'm in for the show!

Can the Future Hear Us?

I waved at the clouds, did you see that affair?
Do they giggle back or just sit in despair?
If I shout my ambitions, will they go far and wide?
Maybe they'll bring me a ride, or a guide!

The future is sneaky, it peeks from behind,
Wearing a mask, seeming jittery and blind.
Will it respond with a wink, or a wave of the hand?
Hey future, are you out there? You've got to understand!

A dog runs past, chasing its tail round and round,
Maybe it knows secrets of joy that abound.
Should I dance with my questions, or sit with my
thoughts?
Do pigeons hold wisdom? Or just care about pots?

I'll keep asking loudly, as loud as I dare,
To see if the future will stop and will care.
With each little chuckle, I'm hopeful and free,
The unknown is funny, oh, what could it be?

Curiosity's Complicated Path

Why do ducks quack at the moon?
Is it a dance or a tune?
Do socks have secret lives?
Or just hide where mischief thrives?

If cats are kings on a throne,
What do they do when alone?
Do they plan their royal schemes?
Or simply nap in cat dreams?

If toast could talk, what would it say?
"Burnt is beautiful, hip-hip-hooray!"
Do we laugh to keep from crying?
Or is it just a way of trying?

Who decided that cheese is great?
Was it a mouse or simply fate?
Could we live without our quirks?
Or is life just a show with perks?

The Paradox of Existence

Is a goldfish lost in its bowl?
Swimming in circles, what's the goal?
Do they ponder great mysteries?
Or just float, hoping for histories?

Why do we count sheep to sleep tight?
Do they hold secrets of the night?
Are we searching for dreams that we miss?
Or just looking for that slumber bliss?

If fireflies blink, what do they say?
"Come join us in our light ballet!"
Are they winking at fate's own game?
Or just flashing their flashy fame?

Could a potato feel quite sly?
If it had a brain, oh my, oh my!
Would it plot against the stew?
Or just chill in the garden's view?

Do Dreams Shape Reality?

If dreams can leap from night to day,
Can they also lead us astray?
Do we follow paths of floating fluff?
Or wake up feeling like, "That's enough!"?

Do the stars whisper wishes in flight?
Or just giggle at our silly plight?
Can wishes turn into wild schemes?
Or are they just the lopsided dreams?

What if rainbows taste like pie?
Would that make clouds give flying a try?
Do rainbows hide flavors we crave?
Or just promise what's soft, sweet, and brave?

Is reality just a big game show?
Where we appear and then say "Hello"?
Are we contestants in life's wild ride?
Or just players with nowhere to hide?

Inquiries at the Edge of Dawn

What's hiding in today's first light?
Is it wisdom or just sheer delight?
Do sunbeams tickle the sleepy heads?
Or stir up thoughts of unsaid dreads?

Why do pancakes flip almost right?
Yet end up stuck in an epic fight?
Do we serve our breakfast with flair?
Or let it flop without a care?

If morning birds gossip at dawn,
Do they chat of dreams now foregone?
Are they plotting a grand serenade?
Or just singing of crumbs laid and made?

Why do we seek answers with glee?
When the best fun is just being free?
Is life a riddle that we will solve?
Or a wobbly dance we constantly evolve?

The Silent Sigh of Infinite Inquiry

Why do socks vanish in the wash?
Is it a dance or just a nosh?
Do bananas see beyond their peel?
Or are they just fruit fare, surreal?

If cats know secrets we don't hold,
Why won't they share, just once, be bold?
Do turtles ponder while they stroll?
And what's the turtle's life goal, on the whole?

When coffee spills, does it lament?
Or is it just an odd event?
Do questions float on wispy dreams?
Or sip from cups in unruly themes?

At midnight, do the stars conspire?
Beneath their glow, do they aspire?
Do we ask too much or not enough?
With life's quirks, it can get tough!

What Stories Do Absences Tell?

Do chairs miss them when they're gone?
Or do they just sit, all forlorn?
When a joke flops, does humor sigh?
Or does laughter just wave goodbye?

What tales weave in empty rooms?
Do clocks still tick in silent dooms?
Are ghosts just lost things trying to play?
Or avoiding the mess of yesterday?

Do whispers echo in empty halls?
Or do they just bounce off walls?
When laughter lands, but nobody's there,
Does it leave a message in the air?

What do shadows say without light?
Do they gossip about the night?
Absences dance, oh, what a show!
Leaving us guessing, where do they go?

Beyond the Horizon of Understanding

Is there a border where thought begins?
Or just a path where confusion spins?
Do thoughts wear hats when out for a stroll?
Or do they trip on their own shoal?

If I ask questions that don't end,
Does my brain just stop and pretend?
Do ants hold meetings beneath the leaf?
Or just plan their day's juicy grief?

Do clouds think deeply before they rain?
Or do they drip just to entertain?
What do trees talk about at night?
Is it gossip about the moonlight?

Are we all lost in a wonder game?
Chasing answers that sound the same?
With each question, do we take a bow?
Or are we just grinning, lost in how?

The Tapestry of Muted Whys

Why do we laugh at the silliest things?
Does joy wear dolls or fancy wings?
If chairs could chat, what tales would they weave?
Or would they just laugh and take their leave?

Do fish ponder in watery streams?
Or do they just swim, chasing dreams?
Are cupcakes sad when they get devoured?
Or do they leap with joy, empowered?

What wisdom lies in the ants' parade?
Do they debate if the sugar's weighed?
Do clouds chuckle at our daily plight?
As they drift softly into the night?

What quirks shape the humor we share?
Is laughter just life's tender affair?
With muted whys that dance and play,
Making sense in a quirky way?

Can the Heart Measure Time?

What if love ticks like a clock?
Can joy dance on the face of a rock?
If laughter grows wings and can fly,
Do we age while we simply sigh?

When dreams slip like shoes off our feet,
Is a heartbeat a rhythm or just a beat?
If wishes come true with a wink,
Should we worry or just overthink?

Can friendship stretch miles with a laugh?
Is life's answer a riddle or a gaffe?
If moments are candy, sweet and sublime,
Do we chew on regret as we muse the rhyme?

In this circus of big and small,
Do we stand tall or trip and fall?
With each question like confetti that swirls,
Are we just kids in this life of whirls?

Unveiling the Veil of Today

Why does Monday wear a frown?
Is Tuesday just a clown in a gown?
If Wednesday winks at the weekend near,
Do we celebrate with a dance or a beer?

Can Thursday complain and still be bright?
Do we spell 'serious' with a giggle or fright?
If Friday hides in a game of charades,
Are our plans just paper masquerades?

When Saturday saunters with a grin,
Is it where our true selves begin?
What if Sunday just wants to nap,
Can we catch dreams in a friendly map?

If today's a puzzle with pieces that flip,
Is it fine to indulge in a silly quip?
Unveiling the layers as we laugh and play,
Isn't life just one wild, funny buffet?

The Beauty of an Open End

What if stories never quite conclude?
Do characters linger, confused or lewd?
If endings are like socks that disappear,
Is the fun in the hunt, or in our cheer?

Can a plot twist compete with a good pun?
Are cliffhangers better than having no fun?
What if journeys are the best gift to send,
Are we all just hoping for an open end?

If sequels become tales of monkey business,
Should we ponder life's a humorous illness?
When characters stumble and trip on fate,
Do we clap and cheer for a twist so great?

In this wide world of pages unturned,
Is the laughter in journeys we've learned?
With a giggle at the trail we extend,
Life's a book with an unexpected send.

Are We Just Reflections?

If mirrors laugh while we do the dance,
Are we shadows caught in a chance?
Can a hiccup bring joy with a snicker?
When we stumble, does laughter grow quicker?

Are we simply jesters in this grand show?
Do our dreams wander where wishes flow?
If reflections wink at the stories we tell,
Is the punchline life wishing us well?

Can we find magic in an echoing hall?
With the right angle, do we stand tall?
If our quirks are just sparkles adorning our fate,
Are we funny shapes on a plate we create?

If life is a riddle we often divide,
Do we wear chaos as a badge of pride?
As we ponder our answers with a giggle or grin,
Are we just echoes of laughter within?

Reflections in a Pool of Questions

Why do socks always lose their mate?
Curious minds ponder fate.
Do fish ever wish to fly?
Or is it just us asking why?

What's the sound of one hand clapping?
Is sleep just reality napping?
If knowledge is power, is ignorance bliss?
Shouldn't that be something we miss?

Do clouds get tired of floating?
And why is the sky always gloating?
Do chairs dream of being sat?
Or is that just an idle chat?

When do hiccups decide to show?
Is it time for a comedy show?
Can we tickle a cactus for fun?
Life's mysteries are never done!

The Symphony of Unasked Queries

If a tree falls and no one's near,
Does it whisper secrets we can't hear?
Do ants hold a parade underground?
Or is their marching just round and round?

Why do we count sheep to sleep tight?
Are they just taking their flight?
If a donut could talk to a cake,
Would they gossip about the mistakes?

Can we ever fit in a square hole?
Or is that just a funny goal?
If happiness were a flavor of pie,
Would we all ask for a slice to try?

Why does the sun like to rise early?
Is it working, or just feeling squirrely?
If questions were jewels, would they shine bright?
Or would they just make us lose sight?

Navigating the Sea of Wonder

Is a jellyfish really not a fish?
Could a goldfish fulfill a wish?
Do lobsters dance when no one's around?
Or do they just sit quietly, profound?

If you tickle a chicken, what does it say?
Does it cluck in a different way?
Are vacuum cleaners really so shy?
Or do they just love to say goodbye?

Do clouds ever argue about their shape?
Can we give them a new escape?
If umbrellas could store raindrops, oh dear,
Would they hope for a warm sunny year?

What's the foot of a mountain, we ask?
Is it just part of a heavy task?
Can rocks be chatty beneath your feet?
Or do they find silence quite a treat?

Capturing Ephemeral Thoughts

What is the sound of a whispering breeze?
Do raindrops giggle when they tease?
If shadows could dance, would they get shy?
Or would they leap and twirl in the sky?

Do cookies dream of being a pie?
And can a sandwich ever tell a lie?
If pencils could paint, what would they draw?
Would it be a masterpiece or just a flaw?

Why do we laugh at the silliest things?
Is joy just the tune that the heart sings?
If the moon invented a midnight snack,
Would it serve marshmallows, piled on a stack?

How many times can one joke be told?
Will laughter ever grow old?
If thoughts are like bubbles that float in the air,
Should we catch them all with utmost care?

The Intersection of Curiosity and Reality

Why does toast always land jam-side down?
Are socks in the dryer having a town?
If cats could talk, what tales would they weave?
And why does the dog think it's fine to grieve?

Is the universe just one big game of charades?
While we stumble through life in our colorful shades?
Do potatoes dream of being hot fries?
Or are they just masters of clever disguise?

What if sleep is just a portal to space?
Where we float with the stars, a cosmic embrace?
Do fish ever ponder the depth and the sea?
Or do they just swim, so blissfully free?

In this funny maze, we laugh and we sigh,
Curiosity's wonder always lifts us high.
So let's chase the absurd, with joy in our stride,
For life's silly riddles are best shared, side by side!

What Is the Shape of Tomorrow?

If tomorrow's a circle, where do we start?
Is it shaped like a pancake or a playdough heart?
When time takes a chance to blur its own line,
Is "now" merely a giant punchline?

Are dreams just balloons waiting for flight?
Should we fill them with giggles, or fears, late at night?
Can laughter be measured—does it come in a cup?
If so, let's fill up and never give up!

What tune does the future hum under its breath?
Is it a dirge or a jingle, a dance with a heft?
When we paint with our whims and our wildest cheer,
Does tomorrow become what we envision here?

As we twirl through the days like a merry-go-round,
Each question a joy, making laughter our sound.
With a brush of absurd, let's color the day,
For the shape of tomorrow is just how we play!

Weaving Whys into Whimsy

Why do we giggle at the silliest things?
Is it just the joy that a good joke brings?
Do shadows have stories they long to relay?
Or are they just shy in the light of the day?

Do clouds sometimes grumble when raindrops get loud?
Is the sun just a spotlight on an invisible crowd?
Can a wish be a puzzle, a flighty device?
Or a tape measure used to count up the nice?

When pigeons parade in their silly grey suits,
Are they planning a dance or just out for shoots?
What does a squirrel say when the nut's out of reach?
Maybe it's a lesson—life's not just a breach!

As we weave these whys with laughter and glee,
The world spins along, such a curious spree.
Each chuckle a thread in this grand tapestry,
Where our whimsy and wonder just set our minds free!

Echoes of the Unasked

Can silence hold secrets like whispers at night?
Do echoes ever giggle at their own delight?
Is the moon just a friend who likes to play coy?
And stars just want us to find our own joy?

What if clouds were really just fluff from a dream?
And rivers were tickled at their own quick stream?
When shadows do leap, do they long for a dance?
Or are they just pranking in a game of chance?

If the sun took a break, would it go for a tea?
And what if the grass could laugh, wild and free?
Time's tick-tock beats bring a grin to our face,
But what of the jokes in the quietest space?

In these echoes of thoughts that we sometimes avoid,
Let's shine a bright light where the giggles are buoyed.
For in every "why" that we choose to pursue,
There's a comedy waiting in the odd and the new!

Can Silence Speak to Us?

In the hush where echoes fade,
Do thoughts dance or do they braid?
Whispers wear a cheeky grin,
Is quiet truly where we begin?

Can silence hold a lively tune?
Or does it plot beneath the moon?
If I shout in a library's maze,
Will the books give me wicked praise?

Mice might laugh in the dark, it's true,
While cats roll eyes as if they knew.
Does pondering make us act less brave?
Or is it just a fancy wave?

With silence, I often misunderstand,
Are giggles hiding in the sand?
If the void wore socks of bright pink,
Would it answer when you think?

The Array of Possibilities at Dawn

At dawn, the choices start to tease,
Coffee or tea? Oh, what a breeze!
Sunrise blushes in golden hues,
Do dreams come with morning's muse?

Birds argue over the worm's delight,
Is breakfast just a fancy fight?
What if toast had something to say?
Would it whisper, 'Eat me, hooray!'?

The sun's a joker, peeking slow,
Does it know where the shadows go?
A squirrel juggles acorns with glee,
Should I ask if it's just like me?

Can choices chase the sleepy haze?
Or do they play hide and seek for days?
With each possibility in sight,
Is every dawn a funny bright?

What Lies Beyond the Expected?

A cat might think it's the king of the lawn,
Or a goldfish dreams of flying at dawn.
What if the grass gives a sigh of relief?
Does it giggle when we're late for our brief?

What's beyond the glassy blue?
Maybe a land of dancing stew?
Do clouds conspire in fluffy debates?
Are rainbows simply chance for mates?

If you open a cupboard, what leaps out?
Could it be a panda who plays with doubt?
The unexpected shows up in guise,
Is it silly, or wise in disguise?

When we wander with curious zest,
Do we uncover life's cheeky jest?
What lies beyond seems wildly fun,
Are we the punchline, or just begun?

The Quest for Meaning in a Fragmented World

In a puzzle with pieces askew,
Do the corners conspire to view?
Is meaning found deep in the cracks,
Or does it wear mismatched socks in packs?

A dog chases tales of its own,
Whispers of wisdom in every bone.
What if laughter is a hidden clue?
Could it be the glue for me and you?

When we search for what surely weighs,
Is life throwing wild cabaret plays?
Fragments giggle and rattle with flair,
Is the quest just life's elaborate hair?

Perhaps meaning's a game we contrive,
Scribbled on napkins, still live and thrive.
In this world, full of pieces and parts,
Are we crafting joy in our hearts?

Searching for Significance in the Ordinary

In the depths of my cereal bowl,
Do I find wisdom, or just soul?
Is that a toy or a hidden clue?
What does the milk say about you?

What's the secret in that peanut shell?
Could it hold the answer—who can tell?
A shoe left behind without its pair,
Is it lonely or just taking air?

Traffic jams turn surreal at best,
Is the honking a grand protest?
Is there meaning in my lost keys?
Or just a sign I should take a breeze?

Each mundane moment calls for fun,
What's the punchline? Come join the run!
Life's a riddle, unravel the yarn,
Chase the ordinary, it won't harm!

Is Certainty an Illusion?

Is the world really straight or just curved?
Do eyebrows raise when truth's unnerved?
If I'm lost, did I ever know?
Or am I just part of the show?

Why does my cat look so profound?
Does he ponder the universe round?
An open window, is it a breeze?
Or a sign I've forgotten my keys?

In a game of chess, what's the best move?
Is it winning, or just finding groove?
Sweaty palms begging for a straight thought,
But the more I grasp, the less I've got!

Oh, how delightful to laugh at doubt,
Finding humor is what life's about!
If certainty walks, it trips on its shoe,
Catch me giggling—it could be you!

What Lies Beneath the Surface?

Beneath the lake, is it truly deep?
Or is it just where the fishes sleep?
What's hiding in that pile of socks?
A secret world or just some rocks?

I ponder on these curious spots,
While sipping coffee, lost in thoughts.
Does the toaster long for some bread?
Or is it plotting to make breakfast dread?

The sky's a blanket, fuzzy and wide,
Is it hiding secrets, or just my pride?
And what's up with the fridge light's glow?
Is it cheering for snacks, or putting on a show?

There's humor in what we seldom see,
Life's mystery wrapped up like a key.
So let's dive deep into giggly quests,
For the best jokes are hidden in jest!

The Space Between What Is and What Could Be

In the gap of thoughts, what do we find?
A ping-pong ball or a wandering mind?
Chasing shadows, is that a new sport?
Or just a fancy way to avoid court?

What happens when plans go awry?
Is it failure in disguise, oh my!
Or a plot twist that's wild and sweet?
Like wearing mismatched socks on your feet?

In the tick-tock between dream and deed,
Do we stumble on laughter or just mislead?
Life's a dance on a crowded floor,
Do we step on toes or just encore?

So linger a moment, enjoy the pause,
The space in between is the real cause.
For what will be holds giggles galore,
So let's keep asking, explore and adore!

The Prelude of a Silent Answer

Why is the sky blue and not a peach?
Do ducks ever wonder what they can teach?
Frogs croak at night, in a curious spree,
Is it the moon or the voice of a tree?

If I chase my shadow, will it run away?
Or does it just linger in a shy ballet?
Pigeons in parks hold secret debates,
Are they planning revolts or discussing their states?

What's the point of cats, lounging on the floor?
Do they contemplate life, or just snore?
An elephant dances, what could it mean?
Is it a circus act, or a dance with a bean?

Am I a philosopher or just feeling silly?
Wondering if laughter is ever too frilly?
Maybe the answer is lost in the air,
Tickled by thoughts that dance everywhere.

A Map of What Might Be

Where does my sock go after the wash?
Does it explore worlds, feeling quite posh?
If cows had dreams, what would they design?
A utopia of grass? Or a place that's divine?

Should I ask the goldfish what he thinks of life?
Does he ponder existence or swim with no strife?
A roadmap for choices is probably neat,
But do we need maps when we have two left feet?

If plants could talk, would they share their views?
Or gossip about neighbors, perhaps sing the blues?
Could I be a cactus or a dainty bouquet?
What's cooler to be on this whimsical day?

Do raindrops have plans as they tumble and fall?
Do they team up, forming a rivulet call?
Perhaps every question's a play in disguise,
Frolicking doubts living under bright skies.

Caught Between Two Worlds

Am I awake or just dreaming a scheme?
Is breakfast a meal or a mystical dream?
If I trip on my shoe, will it laugh in delight?
Or will it just sit there, quiet and polite?

Cats pretend to plot when I'm not around,
Do they giggle at humans, thinking they're profound?
If I ask a squirrel for a dose of advice,
Will it chirp wisdom, or just roll the dice?

Are doors really portals or just simple wood?
Do they harbor secrets misunderstood?
Between dreams and reality, where do I stand?
A plank on the ocean, paddling with one hand?

Cupcakes whisper sweetly, their frosting so bright,
Do they know their fate when they're served at night?
In this mix-up of worlds, it's the humor I seek,
A chuckle, a giggle, perhaps an odd tweak.

The Weight of Unspoken Queries

Why do we worry about socks and their friends?
Are they plotting a journey where the laughter never ends?
If muffins could talk, what tales would they spin?
Would they gossip of crumbs and the chaos within?

Do toasters ever question their daily grind?
Or marvel at bagels, so round and entwined?
If I ask my mirror to share what it sees,
Could it read all my thoughts or just say, 'Cheese'?

Why do clouds float, so free and so grand?
Are they bored of drifting or have they a plan?
If I could ask rainbows what colors they crave,
Would they choose a palette that's bold and brave?

Under the weight of these thoughts, I chuckle with glee,
Life's a riddle wrapped up in a quirky marquee.
If answers elude me or simply run away,
I'll just laugh and dance through this silly array.

What If Time Is a Mirage?

What if clocks just like to play?
Tick-tock dancing all the day.
Seconds skipping, having fun,
Laughing at what we think we've won.

Is noon just lunchtime's disguise?
Or are we all just in a fry?
Wasting minutes, counting sheep,
As tomorrow hides and does not peep.

What if age is just a game?
A number, but none feel the same.
Pirates plunder while we fret,
The treasure's laughter, don't forget!

So let's toast with sweet lemonade,
Time's a friend, let's not invade.
With swirling clocks and giggles bright,
We'll dance and waltz into the night.

The Canvas of Life's Enigmas

What if life's a messy paint?
With colors bold, and dreams that faint.
Splashing joy on canvas bare,
And stealing giggles from the air.

Who needs a line that's straight and true?
When doodling is what we can do?
Each drip and drop's a secret sigh,
A masterpiece that asks us why.

With splatters here and smudges there,
A brush of chaos everywhere.
Life's quirks, oh what a lovely sight,
A gallery of sheer delight!

Let's frame the oddities we find,
Each question mark, to life aligned.
With laughter curling in each bend,
Shall we embrace the art, my friend?

The Threads of Wonder in a Woven Day

What if days are just a weave?
Threading laughter, make-believe.
Twisting tales in every strand,
A tapestry of moments, hand in hand.

What color is a Tuesday's grin?
A polka dot or striped within?
Each hour's pattern plays its part,
With needle wisdom, stitch the heart.

Unraveling yarns of comedy,
Knitting knots of irony.
Woolly thoughts just spinning round,
Making sense of joys profound.

So let's craft with tangled cheer,
These threads of wonder, drawing near.
In every loop and every twist,
A playful life we can't resist!

Is Intuition a Guide or a Trap?

What if gut feelings lead astray?
Whispering secrets in a silly way.
Do we follow, or do we flee?
Is my stomach asking, "Not for me?"

With hunches sharp like a sock with a hole,
Leading me down a path or a shoal.
Should I trust the whims of my mind,
Or listen to reason that's so hard to find?

Is intuition's map all made of cheese?
Or just riddles carried on a breeze?
A compass spinning without a clue,
Telling me what a fool ought to do.

So here's a toast to the nags inside,
Whether as guides or just a wild ride.
Let's laugh at the chances we all take,
With intuition's giggles, let's never break!

The Tightrope of Possibility

I walk a line of dreams and jest,
With each step, I wonder what's best.
Is it the pie or the cake on the shelf?
Or just a nap in the warmth of oneself?

I juggle ideas like oranges bright,
Chasing my thoughts, oh what a sight!
Should I dance with the cat or sing with the dog?
Or start a new hobby like painting a frog?

A thought bubbles up, then it escapes,
Like a balloon filled with all sorts of shapes.
Will I soar high or just float in the breeze?
Life is a puzzle, a playful tease!

So I stroll on this line, feeling alive,
In a circus of choices, I twist and I dive.
With a wink and a grin, I embrace the unknown,
Oh, the tightrope of maybes that I call my own!

Dreams Lost in Questioning

In a world where I ponder and play,
I question my path almost every day.
Should I bake cookies or take a long ride?
Or challenge a squirrel to a playful slide?

My dreams float like clouds, fluffy and light,
But mixed in with worries that nibble and bite.
Should I plant flowers or hunt for a cat?
Life's a buffet; I can't choose what to eat fat!

I scratch my head, wondering what's next,
Should I lounge in my jammies or fix up my texts?
The answers evade like stars in the haze,
While I trip on my socks in a questioning daze!

So I laugh at the mess and grin at the fuss,
In the garden of choices, it's all a big plus.
Lost in my dreams that tickle my mind,
Life is a riddle, whimsical and unkind!

The Labyrinth of Mind and Soul

In a maze of my thoughts, I turn left and right,
With a map that's a doodle, nothing feels right.
Is it the cheese at the end or the fun in the chase?
Or just a strange sock that I can't seem to place?

I tumble through questions, around and around,
Searching for answers that can't be found.
Should I wear mismatched shoes or rock polka dots?
Or simply eat cake while I ponder my thoughts?

The mind is a puzzle, a wild thing to tame,
With every new question, it plays a strange game.
Shall I dance with the moon or sing to the sun?
In this labyrinth, I'm losing my fun!

Yet I giggle and skip through this quirky maze,
Finding joy in the twists and the curious fays.
Life's a riddle wrapped in a raucous delight,
Lost in a lab, but everything feels right!

Unraveling the Thread of Existence

With a needle of laughter, I stitch up my days,
Tying together the most tangled of ways.
Is this a scarf, or a hat gone awry?
Or an art piece made by a curious fly?

I pull at the thread, it dances and swirls,
Each knot a new question, a tumble of pearls.
Should I follow this yarn or get lost in the fog?
Maybe chat with a fish or wrestle a dog?

As I weave in and out of the fabric of fate,
I giggle at chaos, it's never too late.
Do I choose the adventure or stay in my lane?
In the tapestry of life, there's much to gain!

So I unravel and tangle, with mirth in the mix,
With each playful twist, I learn all the tricks.
Life's a grand tapestry, funny and bold,
Every thread a story just waiting to be told!

Do We Measure Depth with Time?

Tick-tock, the clock does rattle,
Are we deep, or just in the battle?
A minute feels like a bitter hour,
As we ponder with existential power.

One thought leads to another twist,
Is that joy, or a fries-dipped mist?
Count the grains in the hourglass,
Or just enjoy a dance with sass.

Should we wear our minds like shoes?
Can they fit, or will they refuse?
We walk on smiles, not on fears,
But how deep are our giggling tears?

In a race with our stubborn thoughts,
Do we win the prize or just the knots?
Time is a joker, full of tricks,
Measure it right, or just get your fix.

The Spaces Between Our Words

Oh, the pauses in our chatter,
Are they glue, or just a scatter?
In the silence, we might find,
The zany thoughts that bind the mind.

Between 'hello' and 'goodbye's flair,
Lies a joke just hanging there.
We trip on tongues and fumble speech,
Yet, strange wisdom is what we reach.

The pauses grow like trees in bloom,
Filling our heads, avoiding gloom.
When we blink and take a breath,
Do we seem alive, or face our death?

A laugh can slip through every crack,
It fills the spaces, brings us back.
So let's chat with goofy glee,
In every gap, let's just be free!

Question Marks in a World of Periods

In a land where dots reside,
We're the question marks with nowhere to hide.
We wobble and dance, looking for facts,
Twirling on whims, dodging the tracks.

Life's a circus, with clowns galore,
Where every answer leads us to more.
So we poke and prod, we tickle and tease,
In a world of full stops, we roam with ease.

When days blend with silly when's,
And logic spins in nonsensical bends,
We might just chuckle at fate's cruel joke,
Finding humor in every woke poke.

Periods march like soldiers in long lines,
While we shimmy past with our quirky signs.
Let's celebrate chaos, the curious spark,
For without a question, where's the lark?

How Do We Know What We Know?

With every 'yes' there's a 'no' to chase,
What's the truth in this dizzy race?
We ask and guess, a game of absurd,
Then laugh at the nonsense we've all heard.

Answers float like feathers in air,
Some wise, some wild, but do we care?
With a poke to the brain and a laugh like a bell,
We spin theories like yarn, and that's just swell.

Reason dances on the edge of wit,
Do we grasp the essence, or just do a split?
Knowledge might wiggle, prance, and gloat,
But are we sailing, or just in a moat?

So we ponder and joke, with whimsical schemes,
Living life like it's all just dreams.
The mystery flavors every fleeting hour,
In every giggle, life's silly power.

The Subtle Art of Wondering

Why does toast always land jam-side down?
Is it fate or just my clumsiness at play?
I ponder why socks vanish without a sound,
Are they off to a party while I'm stuck in gray?

Questions dance like toddlers in the sun,
What if cats are truly plotting our fall?
Could a pineapple be banned from the fun?
At least it wears a crown; that's the call!

Do the stars giggle when I make a wish?
Is the moon simply a big birthday cake?
Or does the universe roll its cosmic fish?
With the answers lost, what choices do I make?

In the end, it's a whimsical routine,
Where thoughts bounce like a rubber ball.
Do we laugh at what we may have seen?
Or just laugh because we might just stall?

Is There Poetry in Uncertainty?

Can a chicken cross the road with flair?
Or is she just chasing her lost sense of pride?
Is there poetry hiding in thin air?
With every twist, the punchline may slide.

Why are ducks such famous pond dwellers?
Do they lead secret lives, quacking away?
What if they're all advanced fortune tellers,
Predicting the weather with each splashing sway?

When will the spaghetti dance come to be?
Is the blueberry muffin a dessert of dreams?
Are we just bubbles floating—wait and see—
Or are all our plans merely fanciful schemes?

In the kitchen of life, no recipe's clear,
Just a pinch of chaos, a dash of zest.
But with laughter around, we have nothing to fear,
As uncertainty gives our slice of life its best.

What Changes When We Ask?

Does the universe favor the curious soul?
Or is it simply whirling away in delight?
If I ask my goldfish, will he take a stroll?
Or splatter his thoughts in bubbles of light?

What of the socks? Do they dream of romance?
Or maybe they just crave a degree of freedom?
If I pose the question, will they take a chance?
And burst forth like superheroes but seldom see them?

When I inquire if my pizza has wings,
Does it laugh at the thought of flying so high?
Are we all just searching for trivial things,
Gathering stories to share, and ask why?

So I question the clouds; do they feel weightless?
Or ponder the raindrops that fall without care?
In the end, it's all about the lightness,
And how laughter can lift the burdens we bear.

Steps on a Pathless Trail

What if paths are merely suggestions, you see?
Are squirrels the true guides of the lost way?
Does their chatter lead us to wild jubilee,
While we stumble in search of a map for the day?

Why does every flower look up with a grin?
Could it be that they just love the sun's play?
As we wander alone, do they welcome us in,
Or are they too busy with their own bouquet?

If I walk backwards, will I meet my past?
Or just find a new route that loops and bends?
What if unicorns existed at last,
And wear sunglasses as they laugh with friends?

Life's quirks are treasures, each twist is a thrill,
When we laugh at the silly, we find our way through.
So dance down that pathless trail with good will,
And let the strange wonders of asking ensue!

In the Quiet of Wondering

Why is cheese so squeaky at night?
Does the moon wear pajamas or put up a fight?
If cats could talk, would they be terse?
Or draft a novel that's truly diverse?

Do clouds get tired of floating around?
And does ice cream feel cold on the ground?
If I wear socks with sandals today,
Will the fashion police take me away?

Where do socks go, when they disappear?
Can laughter be bottled and sold by the year?
If fish could surf, would they ride the tide?
Or is the ocean their own joyride?

What if grass could make a sharp remark?
Would trees whisper secrets that hit the park?
In this world of wonder and quirky spree,
How many questions are waiting for me?

The Synthesis of Inquiry and Experience

Is cereal soup with a crunch to it?
Or does a donut dismiss the true wit?
Do penguins wear tuxedos to tease?
Or do they just waddle with utmost ease?

Can you tickle a fish, or would it flee?
And does a cactus laugh, humming with glee?
If toaster strudels are the breakfast kings,
Do waffles play chess with syrupy swings?

What if your shoes woke up and danced?
Or if cats held parties, would we be pranced?
In a world where questions dance like a jig,
What's the answer, my big furry pig?

Are ducks just chickens that swam a mile?
And do potatoes dream of being in style?
The spirit of fun keeps asking for more,
What else could be knocking at inquiry's door?

Shades of Ambiguity

Is a pickle a fruit, or merely a tease?
Can clouds breathe deeply, or do they wheeze?
If carrots could speak, would they sing a tune?
Or ponder why we all love the moon?

Do mirrors have stories they refuse to tell?
And can shadows giggle? Would that be swell?
If spaghetti had arms, would it try to hug?
Or just twirl around like a charming bug?

What if books had thoughts and dreams at night?
Would they confide in the quirky starlight?
A world of puzzling quirks struts with pride,
As we unravel these thoughts side by side.

Why do we ponder what all of this means?
Could a sheet of paper really dream of beans?
With each chuckle, new questions arise,
Peering through laughter, oh what a surprise!

Moments Suspended in Inquiry

Does toast get jealous of the crusty bread?
And do raindrops gossip about what they said?
If a chair could dance, would it leap and sway?
Or would it just sit back and call it a day?

Can a cupcake be serious with sprinkles on top?
And what do pillows do when we stop?
If bananas could talk, would they share a pep?
Or sit in silence, still dreaming of step?

What if a snail ran a fast food stand?
Would customers laugh, or give him a hand?
In this buoyant dance of wonder and jest,
How we giggle at questions, life's little quest.

Why can't we hoot like an old wooden owl?
Or ride bicycles made of a fluffy towel?
In each playful riddle, there's magic to find,
With laughter as anchors, we're one of a kind!

Whispers of Uncertainty

Why does toast always land butter-side down?
Are socks in the dryer waging a war?
Is that my sandwich or a ball from a clown?
Where did my other shoe go – I implore!

Do cats believe they control the whole house?
Can fish truly be bored in their glass dome?
Is my life a sitcom with laughs, like a spouse?
Why does my chair feel like an old, lost throne?

Is the fridge really a portal to munchies?
Should I trust the GPS that's really just lost?
Why does my coffee taste like sad, crunchy sponges?
Am I doomed to wander – just count the cost?

What if dreams are just reruns of our youth?
Do we laugh to mask all the chaos within?
Is a swing set a portal to searching the truth?
Where's the manual for life's great, curious spin?

Shadows of Inquiry

Why do we park our cars in driveways, so neat?
Where do crayons go when they just don't fit?
Is cereal a soup if it's soggy and sweet?
Will my dog judge me for sitting a bit?

What's the secret to finding a matching sock?
Is my plant plotting to overrun the chair?
If I ask my goldfish, will it mock?
Do clouds gossip about how I wear my hair?

Do walls have ears or just very big mouths?
Are puddles portals to the land of the lost?
What's that smell? Oh, it's just my sister's new blouse.
Do I really need to know what it's cost?

Is a taco a sandwich? The world wants to know!
Will the moon stand still for a selfie, I dare?
If time is money, why am I always so slow?
Does chaos come packaged, or is it free air?

The Curiosity of Existence

Why do we feel a tickle when we laugh?
Can a plant's feelings bloom, or is it fake?
Is my cat the boss, holding secret staff?
Where's the direction in the cake I bake?

What's behind door number one – let's just peek!
Could it be danger or a pair of clean shoes?
If I sing in the shower, will the water speak?
Is hiccuping really a great way to lose?

Does my pillow cast dreams when I am asleep?
Can jellybeans really be classified as art?
Why's there a dance party in my head so deep?
Are birthdays just invites for cake to depart?

Is my umbrella plotting my next wet feat?
Will my goldfish take notes when I'm trying to share?
When does adulthood start? Can I get a receipt?
Is the alarm clock a friend or a glare in my chair?

Pondering the Unknown

Where do thoughts go when they disappear?
Is my pen a magician, creating some doubt?
Can time be eaten like candy, oh dear?
What's the remote control got so loud about?

Why can't I ever find the end of the tape?
Is the universe filled with socks that won't play?
If I shout at the stars, will they help me escape?
Do clouds count sheep while they drift in ballet?

What's the recipe for spontaneous fun?
Should I count my mistakes or just brush them away?
Can I dance with my shadow, or must I run?
Is tomorrow just today wearing a toupee?

Do we live in a sitcom, or is it a gag?
Will my morning coffee tell me some lore?
If I tickle my brain, will it laugh or just brag?
Is the meaning of life lost in the drawer?

The Unanswered Echo

Is that a question or a sneeze?
The universe giggles with ease.
Why do socks vanish in the wash?
Did they make a run, or just a posh?

Is my cat plotting my demise?
Or just staring with mischievous eyes?
Do donuts dream of being whole?
Or are they happy, playing their role?

Does the moon wear pajamas at night?
And does it turn off its own light?
Is that a bird or just my brain?
Why does it dance in such a rain?

I asked a fish for some advice,
All it did was mumble and splice.
Life's a riddle wrapped in a song,
Maybe asking is where we belong.

Pondering the Unseen Canvas

What color is the sound of cheese?
Does it dance in the air or just sneeze?
If my thoughts had legs, where would they roam?
Chasing the cat or looking for home?

Can laughter weigh more than a ton?
Or is it free like the morning sun?
Do we paint with our toe or our nose?
Or does it depend on where the wind blows?

Is that a rainbow or just a trick?
Can happiness come in a single flick?
If life's a game, am I in the match?
Or just a player with a mismatched scratch?

When is breakfast over, who sets the clock?
And why do bananas wear a fuzzy frock?
In this house of wonders, we all convene,
With our wild ideas of what life might mean.

Is Tomorrow a New Beginning?

Is tomorrow just Monday in disguise?
Or a date that wears glittery ties?
When does now start and then just fade?
Is it a parade or an escapade?

When coffee spills, is it a brew of fate?
Or just a morning that's running late?
Will my alarm clock learn to compete?
And why do my shoes always leave me on repeat?

If I had a button to reset the day,
Would it make me dance or just delay?
Can a nap bring wisdom like a book?
Or do dreams just tease with a sly little look?

Is today a gift or a mystery box?
With surprises inside that just talk?
Maybe life's a riddle we're meant to keep,
With questions that tickle us just before sleep.

Whispers of the Unsung Journey

Do the stars gossip about our plans?
Or do they just dance with quiet hands?
If clouds could talk, what jokes would they tell?
Would they giggle or laugh, in their fluffy shell?

Is time a trickster, or just a fool?
Playing hopscotch on a cosmic pool?
When do we finish what's been begun?
Or is life like a race where we all just run?

If trees could walk, where would they go?
To a party or just play in the snow?
Do whispers echo in the summer breeze?
And do daisies really aim to please?

Are rainbows lessons from the sky?
Or just dreams that wink as they fly?
In this journey, each twist, each turn,
Is perhaps a question we're meant to learn.

9 781805 660224